Successful Fundraising for Schools

A handy guide to fundraising activities and events to help raise money for schools and similar organisations.

www.successfulfundraisingforschools.co.uk

By Tracey Fowler

Successful Fundraising for Schools

This is a book is packed with simple fundraising ideas and details of how to successfully bring those ideas to fruition.

Copyright © 2013 Tracey Fowler – Twilight Publishing

Cover by Annabel Kingston

CreateSpace

Nonfiction/Reference/Fundraising

First Edition Printing April 2013

ISBN-13: 978-1481898553

ISBN-10: 1481898558

www.successfulfundraisingforschool.co.uk

CONTENTS

Dedicated to my late father, from whom I gained much spirit!

ACKNOWLEDGMENTS

Over the years it has been a joy to be involved in so many community activities, helping to raise funds for and the profile of causes close to my heart. Through this I have gained valuable experience, met some very interesting people and made some lifelong friends.

Organising and taking part in fundraising activities at St Peter's C of E Primary School in Portishead near Bristol over the past ten years has been an enriching experience. My thanks go to staff, parents, pupils and friends who have supported me throughout, especially with some of my more whacky ideas. I have loved every minute of it!

Special thanks to my family: my mum, my husband Derrick and children Jagger and Skye, who have been coerced in to every fundraising activity possible and experienced sitting up until midnight wrapping prizes for a lucky dip, baking cakes at 6am before school and much more, all in the name of fundraising.

I am proud that by the age of 10, both of my children could organise a school fair standing on their heads and aren't afraid to approach people to ask them to buy raffle tickets or programmes for a good cause.

There are also a few special friends, who I won't list, but who know who they are. They need to be thanked for picking me up off the floor when I have been on my knees, when things haven't quite gone according to plan!

And Nick, without the associated website, this book would not be as comprehensive or as helpful to its readers, so thank you.

To acknowledge the rewarding experience I have gained working as part of St Peter's Parent Teacher Association (PTA) and to ensure my contribution to the school continues long after my youngest moves on to secondary education, a donation from the sale of each copy of this book will be made to St Peter's PTA.

Introduction

Successful fundraising for schools, clubs and community groups is more important and more appreciated than ever these days.

There are many books and websites offering help with fundraising ideas and products, but it can take so long to navigate these websites and feedback your findings to a committee and all involved.

Searching for ideas, reading, taking notes and then presenting them to a committee at the next meeting for consideration can be a lengthy process and my motivation for writing this book is to cut that time for you.

This book not only provides a variety of fundraising ideas, but also details of how to bring those ideas successfully to fruition. It shares with you some of the experiences gained in more than 30 years of fundraising and also details of organisations that offer some great products and services to help you in your quest to support your school.

In addition, there are ideas of how to get more volunteers on board and how to promote your events to the wider community.

Presented in a comprehensive handbook, this handy reference book can travel easily with you to committee meetings and can be passed on to new committee members, year in, year out.

Website

The website www.successfulfundraisingforschools.co.uk has been created to use alongside this book. It provides easy access to downloadable letters, forms and notices relating to the activities featured in this publication. There are also sections offering advice on marketing, how to make the best of free press and publicity, along with examples, where to look when seeking sponsorship, details of organisations that offer grant aid and companies that offer support to charitable groups and good causes.

The website also provides a direct contact for me, should you wish to discuss any of the information contained within this book or share any new ideas with me and the fundraising community.

Background Information

I started fundraising at the age of eight, my cause usually being whatever the latest Blue Peter Appeal was. As a child I was also a member of the NSPCC. School holidays were filled with organising jumble sales, teddy bears' picnics and sending out invitations to the rest of the street, asking residents to visit our garage (for a fee of course) which had been turned in to anything from a theatre to a haunted house!

It wasn't until later in life that I became involved in community fundraising for causes like the local youth club and then eventually when I became a mum, I realised how vital Parent Teacher Associations and their fundraising are. Providing items for school, which the Local Education Authority can't cover, can enrich school life for pupils. In our case this ranged from a baby grand piano and musical instruments for free class lessons, to playground equipment and the subsidy of school outings to make them more affordable for everyone.

I was made chairman of the PTA within a year of my eldest child starting school and that's when I realised how many organisations were out there with great ideas and products to help with fundraising.

Every single day there would be letters waiting in my tray, telling me about a product or organisation that could help us raise more money. Investigating these businesses was time consuming though and I could never get through them all.

Committees come and go; so with the best will in the world I would try to file all the letters and catalogues so that when a new committee was elected the following year, the information could be passed on (little did I know I would be sitting in the chair for more years than I care to remember!). I would print off all the ideas emailed to me and file those too, but eventually, so vast was the flow of marketing material from all these different organisations, that the filing took hours of my time every week. In fact, it took up so much time that in the end I rarely got round to reading the letters and emails, let alone start trailing around all the websites to find out more.

My experience of regular meetings, research amongst parents and staff and putting as many fundraising projects as I could manage in to practice, has allowed me to build a comprehensive catalogue of fundraising tips and ideas. I am keen to share all these with other likeminded people who are just as eager as I was to raise funds for good causes.

Using the products and services of many of the different organisations also proved a big learning curve, especially discovering that cheapest doesn't always mean best. Finding the organisations most suitable for your needs is important, especially if you are embarking on a project you have not tried before. The organisations willing to spend time to talk and explain things to you when you have a query and finding a team that will help you when things go wrong are just as important as your profit margin. Remember, making fundraising fun is important and you want to be able to do it with as little stress as possible,

Just to give you some idea of the platform I worked from, our primary school had around 400 pupils, a PTA committee of 12 (most years) and a team of approximately 30 volunteers who were a constant support. Other volunteers tended to sign up to help at just one or two events each year, while others needed a bit of arm twisting!

Members of staff are always very busy, but in my case building a good relationship with them resulted in all members of staff contributing to events and activities at some point during the year. This had a very positive effect on fundraising for our school.

I hope you find this book useful and inspirational and long may your fundraising be successful!

Tracey Fowler

Getting Started

Putting together a plan for your fundraising for the year is a great way to get started. Nothing has to be set in stone, but good planning is essential. If you overcrowd the diary with fundraising events you could find that you spread voluntary help, outside support and people's budgets a bit too thinly.

Having a focus for much of your fundraising is also important. Whilst it's great to subsidise trips or buy the school television licence or Christmas tree, research shows that people tend to dig deeper in to their pockets when the fundraising is for something specific, items that excite them, which they can see the children will benefit from. So draw up a school wish list and prioritise the needs.

When looking for sponsorship or support from the wider community, aim for something specific when pitching your request. So if you are looking to buy a new piano, you may first want to approach organisations with an interest in music. You may even find that celebrity musicians will support your cause with signed photos or memorabilia that you can auction or raffle. If you want to give the school cookery room a makeover, organisations with an interest in food and nutrition may be your first point of call. Local restaurants and cafes may well contribute by donating vouchers offering free meals as prizes.

Remember, even parents and pupils are often more interested in supporting events when they know exactly where the money is going. So if you are asking them to buy raffle tickets or support a sponsored walk; let them know what the proceeds will buy for the school and more importantly, how it will benefit their child/ren.

For future reference make sure you keep a record of your events, what was included, what made the most money, what seemed to give the most enjoyment and the contact details of volunteers so that you can ask them to help again.

You are going to need lots of willing volunteers to help with your fundraising events so keeping the fun in fundraising is very important. If you can make meetings, preparation and the delivery of events fun and interesting you are more likely to get the support you need. Motivating a team and making it a pleasant experience for all involved is very important. If you are enjoying yourself, others will too. Make it a social activity for the organisers as well as hard work!

Your local council will advise on whether you need licences or certificates for your events and activities. This can range from a lotteries licence, events or alcohol licenses to food and hygiene certificates. I can't stress enough how important it is to contact them before you begin planning any events to find out what is required by law and for best practice.

PTA-UK is also there to help and offer advice. PTA-UK is a national charity and membership organisation supporting the PTA market in England, Wales and Northern Ireland. It provides support and practical resources and can be found at www.pta-uk.co.uk.

Risk Assessments

Any activity that can present a risk or injury needs a risk assessment to be carried out and documented. This helps you to think about any possible dangers and how you will overcome them. Your school should be able to help you produce this, the successfulfundraisingforschools website has examples to help you and the Health and Safety Executive website can also provide advice, as can PTA-UK. Risk assessments should be kept for your records and can also be used for future events with a bit of 'tweaking'.

Marketing

Getting customers through the door is what fundraising activities and events are all about. So marketing is a very big part of your fundraising. Sending out newsletters (by electronic mail and/or hard copy in book bags) to parents and carers is a great way to publicise your PTA activities, however experience has taught me that some school families don't get around to reading the correspondence for months. Therefore, posters around school, talking to people at drop off and pick up times, asking teachers if you can visit their classes to give a talk to pupils to get them excited about the events and generally creating a buzz about what is being organised helps enormously.

That takes care of in-house publicity but what about reaching the wider community? You really don't want to be spending money on advertising events so take advantage of any free publicity you can get.

Community newspapers and magazines will always be interested in your news if you present information concisely and in an interesting 'newsy' way. It will be even better received if there is a good photograph to go with it. Post publicity is a good idea too, to keep your cause in the public eye and rally support, so it's worth a call to your local rag to ask them if they can send a photographer along. If they can't, take your own and email it to them with a few lines about what happened at the event and how much money it raised. See if your local radio stations will plug your events and don't forget to put posters up around town. Local shops will usually support you by displaying a poster in their windows.

If your cause will benefit from being in the public eye and you want to raise the profile beyond that of usual activities, it's worth considering an attempt to smash world record as you go about your fundraising. With our help, St Peter's became the Guinness World Record holders for the biggest tombola! The press coverage was amazing which prompted more support. Not only did we receive hundreds of donations of prizes from members of the community and further afield, all willing us to successfully break the record, but we also had hundreds more visitors than usual on the day, all hoping to bag a bargain! Businesses, individuals, clubs and organisations, our local MP and a couple of locally based celebrities all pitched in to help us achieve the record which raised thousands of pounds for our baby grand piano.
Now there's a challenge for you!

Achieving the world record involves a great deal of work because of the rules which include the need for controllers and the production of evidence. So to create some hype for a fair, but to avoid all the extra work of a world record attempt, you could always aim to hold the biggest ever lucky dip or alternative activity your town has seen. It would be sure to catch the eye of the local community and the media and attract plenty of publicity and support.

Be creative in your marketing approach and make the most of any free publicity available. Make sure you know copy deadline dates for your local press so that you don't miss out on a media opportunity.

Recruiting Volunteers

If you are reading this book, the chances are you have already discovered good reasons to join a school Parent Teacher Association (PTA). The secret now is to pass on those good reasons to other people to encourage more volunteers.
Many people think they pay their taxes and so the government should provide everything their children need at school, but the reality is that budgets at every school are tight. Money raised from fundraising activities can be used to pay for extras that can make a difference to the pupils' school days experience.

Helping with PTA events and activities can help build closer relationships with teachers and members of staff too and it can give you a better insight to the way the school works.
Being a part of the PTA can also help you get to know other parents and their children. Talking to other parents, sharing experiences and parenting tips can help everyone. I have made some solid friendships through PTA activities that I know will last long after my children have left school.

Taking part in PTA activities shows your children that you are taking an interest in their school and are sharing their experience. Everyone has different skills they can bring to the PTA and there are always opportunities to develop new skills.

I know a mum who didn't work in paid employment while her children were at primary school but who was an active PTA member for more than 12 years. When her children were older she set up her own successful events management company based on the skills and knowledge she had gained with the PTA.

Lack of confidence can stop some people volunteering but once they have tried it they often enjoy contributing and come back for more. So gentle encouragement to get someone to spend half an hour on a stall can easily develop in to the securing of a long term, valued helper.

It can be very useful to set up some after school workshops to encourage volunteers. These can involve a range of activities. One of my favourites was our annual face painting workshop. We had one or two mums who were fantastic at face painting and they shared their skills by teaching other parents and friends during a one hour workshop. It was always full of laughter (helped along by a glass or two of wine) but over the years resulted in the building of a great face painting team for our school fairs and fetes. With a constantly growing confident army of face painters, we were able to organise a rota at events so that our creative volunteers needed only to sign up for half an hour slots, leaving them free to enjoy the event with their families for the rest of the time.

Other workshops we found extremely worthwhile included biscuit and cake decorating, arts and crafts and team building games, but there is nothing to stop you organising workshops for absolutely any activity, even selling raffle tickets! There is always a way to improve performance to maximise sales, from dressing up to making and wearing sandwich boards.

Most PTAs have monthly meetings. Keep these open to all wherever practical, letting all parents and carers know they are welcome. Make sure you have an agenda and know what you want to achieve from your meeting, but ensure people are encouraged to have their say and try to include time for socialising either at the beginning or end of the meetings.

Setting up a PTA information stall at events provides a great opportunity for parents to find out more and maybe sign up for future events. It's a great way to promote the work of the PTA.

If you haven't yet discovered the joy of helping your school's PTA please consider it now. It's a great way to help schools and pupils and it also helps build the sort of communities we all want to live in.

LET THE FUNDRAISING BEGIN!

FETES AND FAIRS

How to raise thousands!

I am dedicating more space to 'fetes and fairs' than any other one fundraising event or activity because these are often major fundraisers at schools. They also take in numerous activities under their umbrella which can also be run on their own or as part of other events.

Spring fairs, summer fetes, autumn bazaars and Christmas fairs tend to be favourite fundraisers, but what can make the difference between them raising a few hundred pounds and raising thousands?

The size of your school can have some affect on the amount you raise, but the sky's the limit with an event like this, there is no reason why these events can't attract the wider community. If your school is very small you can always move your event to an alternative venue to help it be more lucrative.

Remember, success isn't just measured by the amount of money raised, it's also about the enjoyment people experience while they are parting with their hard earned cash! Make sure your fetes and fairs have a wide variety of stalls and activities so that they have something that will appeal to everyone and ensure people feel they have had value for money. Be sensible when setting prices so that everyone can have a great time and feel they have had their money's worth.

Good, free publicity in the local papers will help to encourage visitors, as will posters in shop windows, the use of social media and general networking. Invitations to sheltered accommodation blocks, retirement homes and other local organisations can also bump up the numbers.

Inviting 'outside' community groups involved in music, dance or sport to perform at your event can help attract even more visitors and if you can manage to persuade a celebrity to open your fair, you could even have to consider the need for crowd control!

Some schools dedicate the main hall for these events but if you can open up the whole school, or at least other parts of it, there is much more chance of exceeding your fundraising expectations. In good weather using outside space is a must, but always have a plan B in case of rain.

Countdown to the Fair

The more support you receive from parents and friends of the school for your fairs and fetes, the more money it will raise for school and the more enjoyable it will be for all those who attend.

A month or so before your event it's a good idea to send out a "Countdown to the Fair" letter. This informs everyone when and where the fair will take place and explains how much support it needs. Make sure everyone knows that all donations you ask for are voluntary and no-one is expected to respond to all requests, as you will be asking for a lot. Then as the event draws nearer hold a soft toy donation day, a bottle donation day, an empty jam jar day, hold a non school uniform day in exchange for tombola prizes and ask people to bake cakes etc. Hold short weekly meetings at the end of the school day to encourage helpers and support for all the donations you will be looking for. Find a team of outgoing people to talk to local businesses to gain their support for extra prizes and sponsorship.

Appoint volunteers for each category so that someone takes care of the jam jars, while someone else washes the soft toys.

Make sure you check the date on any food items and discard any that will be out of date by the day of your event.

Admission Fee

Charging an entrance fee for fetes and fairs is common and a great way to kick off your fundraising, but charging too much may put people off. It's a good idea to keep the admission fee low and allow children in free of charge. People feel they are getting a good deal before they get through the door that way. We always opted for 50p admission but other local schools successfully charge £1.

The Raffle or Draw

The raffle or draw can raise hundreds of pounds even before the fair begins!

First you need at least three great prizes, often seasonal prizes go down well. Weekend breaks, a gas barbecue or family tent for raffles drawn early in the year and perhaps Christmas hampers or cash prizes for the winter events.

If you are only going to sell raffle tickets at the fair you can use cloakroom tickets as long as you draw it at the event at which you are selling the tickets. If however (and this can reap huge rewards) you print draw tickets in advance and sell them ahead of the fair you will need to be registered under the Lotteries Act – contact your district council for help with this.

Approaching local businesses to sponsor or donate the prizes can give them good PR exposure. Make sure you mention their support in the event programme and on posters, tickets etc. and even in the local press. Your friendly, local reporter is sure to be interested in a good news story for the paper's business pages. Our local estate agent Reeds Rains is run by a parent at school, who always offered support. Every year they would generously donate a £100 hamper for the Christmas draw and we would send a photograph to the local press of the agent handing over the goods to pupils. The following week, if we were lucky, the local paper would publish our story with the headline "Local estate agent donates hamper" with the photo alongside. It provided great publicity for our event and was good for Reeds Rains too (our website shows examples of successful press photos). If the prizes are donated, all proceeds from ticket sales are profit for the school – a great start to your event.

Don't promise any publicity you can't guarantee, but discuss the possibilities with local businesses that support you and always remember to write to thank them afterwards. It shows your appreciation and may result in more support in the future.

Printed draw tickets will usually have room for you to include the sponsor. They will come in books of 5 or 10 and a book or two can be sent home with pupils via their book bags a week or two prior to your event. Make sure you print on the ticket when and where the draw will take place, the details of the registered promoter and your cause information. Most ticket printing organisations will guide you with the necessary information. Ask for completed counterfoils and money to be returned to the school office by a certain date, along with any unsold tickets. More tickets can be sold at the event.

On the day make sure your ticket sellers are full of confidence and enthusiasm. Walking around the fair in brightly coloured costumes selling the tickets will work much better than someone standing behind a table with a pile of tickets in front of them.

Trade or craft stalls

Another way to make money before your event begins is to sells space to local crafts people or small businesses. How many outside stalls you invite will depend on the space you have available, but if you offer 10 stands to independent organisations and charge them £10 or £15 each, it gives you at least £100 in the bank before you begin your fair. It would be usual to provide a table for your invited traders.

You can advertise the spaces and your terms in the school newsletters – it's surprising how many parents run small or part-time businesses. Entrepreneurs producing their own wares and services are often delighted to participate in these events. Alternatively, if it's for a good cause, local media will usually support you with a few lines appealing for stall holders to join you, or of course you could send personal invitations to carefully selected businesses and organisations.

Tombola

As already mentioned, the tombola can be a record breaking activity and a major fundraiser.

A non school uniform day in return for a tombola prize from each pupil the day before your event is the easiest way to accumulate prizes. But asking local shops and businesses to help with prizes, appeals for unwanted gifts from parents, other family members and even neighbours can also be a good boost.

Using a book of cloakroom tickets, label your prizes with the tickets ending in 0 or 5 folding the matching tickets and all the other numbers and placing them in a number of containers.
People pay to have a go and draw tickets from the containers hoping to pull out a ticket ending in 0 or 5 to win the prize that corresponds with their ticket.

Hook a duck or snowman

A paddling pool filled with plastic ducks or shelves lined with plastic bottles faced with a printed image of a snowman, Santa or even the head teacher will do the trick here. You will also need some bamboo canes and either hooks and 'eyes' from the local DIY shop or some magnets. Secure the hooks or magnets on to the canes and 'eyes' or magnets to the ducks or bottles. Put numbers on the bottom of each duck or bottle and display a poster detailing which numbers are winners.

You will need some small prizes for the winning numbers and it's nice to have a bowl of sweets handy so that the losers can help themselves to a consolation prize. If you need to buy the prizes rather than receive donated items, you need to make sure you spend less than you are charging per go. So if you buy a prize for 10p perhaps charge 20p a go. Remember not every go will be a winner so you should be 'quids' in. Alternatively, it is worth approaching local sweet shops, discount stores, wholesalers and supermarkets to ask for prize donations. Free gifts from magazines and fast food restaurants can be saved all year round to use as prizes too.

Grotto

Santa's grotto is very popular at Christmas fairs but using the same idea, you can always switch to a fairy garden or character set for other times of the year.

You will need a dedicated classroom or perhaps the staff room for this activity. You will need several hours to set up, to make the room as magical as possible for the young visitors. Using a pop up gazebo and fairy lights can help create the atmosphere. If you have any artistic volunteers ask them to create scenery and props to accompany your theme.

You will need at least two, preferably more, volunteers to be your main character. It can get very hot inside costumes and swapping volunteers every half an hour is a good idea. You also need some helpers in costumes, like elves for Santa's grotto, or fairies to accompany the fairy queen. These helpers greet your visitors, keep a track of the schedule and make sure everyone has paid.

If it's a Christmas grotto you can include a gift, let's say a £1 selection box. This should be taken in to account when costing tickets. Tickets should be sold in advance and entered on to a timetable so that 10 minute slots are allocated to groups of four or five.

Again, if it's a Christmas grotto, packs of porridge oats in a colourful packet or envelope can be sold or given as reindeer food. Another favourite is coloured stars which can be scattered in the bedroom before bed on Christmas Eve which shine to show Santa how good the children have been. There are lots of variations, just use a bit of imagination.

We charged £2.50 for Santa's grotto which included a £1 selection box, so £1.50 per person was profit.

With modern technology, a photograph option can be introduced. With parents' permission photos can be taken with the special guest. A collection time is given and the photos can be printed out and sold to parents at the end of the fair as a lasting memory.

Teddy Shy

So many households have an abundance of quality soft toys, some of which they are only too pleased to part with when an opportunity presents itself. Putting out an appeal for unwanted quality soft toys often produces a mass of them!

A quick wash and brush up can make them look and smell like new and the teddies can then be used for prizes for lots of activities at the fair. One popular stall is the teddy shy. This is just like a coconut shy but with soft toys not coconuts! Teddies sit on posts while customers pay to throw three bean bags to try and knock them off their seat. If they knock the teddy off, they keep it and it is replaced by another donated toy.

To keep costs down, the tubes from the centre of carpet rolls, cut to different lengths and stood on end, make ideal posts on which to sit the soft toys. Carpet shops are usually willing to donate these free of charge. They can be decorated to make the stall more eye catching.

Tin Can Alley

With a little imagination a tin can alley can produce a great deal of interest. A table is stacked with a number of empty cans built in to a pyramid and customers pay a small amount (we always charged 20p) to throw three bean bags at them, to see how many they can knock down. Scores are registered and the person with the highest score at the end of the event wins a prize. The prize is usually something donated by a local store and a sign is displayed naming the sponsor of the stall. Alternatively you can purchase a prize and deduct the cost from the takings of the stall. If people have the same score there is a play off. Put a sign up saying that any play offs will take place 15 minutes before the end of the event.

The more interesting you make this stall, the more money you can take. One of the most successful tin can alley stalls we ran was one with a Dr Who theme. The person organising it had Dr Who themed music playing to attract attention and of all the cans were faced with photos of different Dr Who characters including the Daleks and Cybermen. Others that have proved extremely popular include Tim Cam Alley, which displayed faces of Timmy Mallett just after he had appeared on the TV show 'I'm a Celebrity' and one that had faces of all the teachers on the cans.

Lucky Dip

Everyone loves a lucky dip. You can run one for adults and a separate one for children, but it is called lucky dip so people do have to take their chances!

All year round I saved any free gifts that came my way from fast food restaurants, magazines etc. and ask friends and neighbours to do the same. We would make a quick plea midterm, via the PTA newsletter, for suitable lucky dip prizes for future events and put them away in the school cupboard. This worked well and worked better than leaving it until the month of the event when parents and friends are concentrating on requests for larger donations like the soft toys and tombola prizes.

Make sure members of staff know that you are on the lookout for prizes too, they can sometimes get overlooked in the hunt for prizes.

Pick a Bottle

A cardboard bottle carrier from the local supermarket covered in wrapping paper is ideal for this stall. You will need six identical bottles, also wrapped in paper and on the bottom of one you need to put a gold star. People pay to pick up a bottle and if they select the one with the star on the bottom they win a prize (usually a bottle!). If they pick one of the five without a star, they lose.

Bottles of grape juice or flavoured fizzy water are ideal for the under 18s and bottles of wine for over 18s. Obviously more profit will be gleaned if you can persuade your local supermarkets to donate some of the bottles and don't forget to display who sponsored the event or donated prizes. The prizes can look extremely attractive if they are wrapped in cellophane with coloured ribbon to top them off.

Guess the Teacher

Guess the teacher games create lots of fun for pupils and parents. You can erect a stand and cover it with photos of teachers but cover parts of their faces by using reindeer masks or Santa masks. Alternatively you can use baby photos or wedding photos.

Answer sheets to fill in are bought for 20p and are completed during the fair and returned to a post box set up especially for them. Before the end of the fair the answers are revealed and all winning entries get a small prize. Prizes can be donated or sponsored gifts can be used, alternatively small 10p bars of chocolate or packets of sweets costing less than the entry fee (to ensure a profit) can be used.

A different spin on this game is guess which pet belongs to which member of staff.

Refreshments

With the volume of people at your fair, it can get very warm, no matter what the time of year. This can leave people feeling very thirsty. It can also be tiring trawling the stalls and activities, especially with a team of small children. A quiet area where people can sit down and have a cup of tea or glass of squash is essential and can be very lucrative. Introducing hot and cold drinks, cakes, biscuits and even lunches, depending on the time of your fair, can be a good earner. A barbecue is another great idea but ensure you adhere to all health and safety rules.

You will need a team of volunteers to prepare the refreshments, others to serve and others to wash up.

You will need to check with your local council for help to ensure you meet food hygiene rules and regulations. If you decide to introduce mulled wine or a bar facility you will need to apply for a licence in advance of your event. Again you need to contact your local council.

Balloon Race

To hold a balloon race you will need a large number of helium filled, biodegradable balloons, some tags and a great prize. For a fee entrants buy a balloon which has a numbered ticket attached. The balloons are released and the buyer of the balloon that travels the furthest and has its ticket returned to the organiser is the winner. You can buy readymade kits to run a balloon race or make your own.

Inflatables

For many years we shied away from hiring in bouncy castles and similar inflatables, worried about health and safety risks. However we discovered that the companies providing them have very strict rules to help ensure everyone stays safe and as long as these are followed they can be used to provide a great deal of enjoyment. We usually found a sponsor to pay for the hire so the takings were all profit in the bank.

Spin and Win

We were lucky enough to recruit a few handy dads on to the PTA. One of which made us a very popular game for us to bring out at fairs.

An easel type construction held a wooden circle like a clock and an arrow. The clock was divided in to 12 numbered sections and we had corresponding numbered vouchers. People bought a number and were given the voucher with their number on. Once 12 numbers had been sold at 50p each we spun the arrow and whichever number it stopped on, the person holding that number won a bottle. We sometimes ran adult only games with bottles of wine as a prize, but largely the bottles were grape juice wrapped in coloured cellophane and tied with a bow. It looked great, the cellophane would contain any glass if the bottle was dropped and it only cost around £1 per bottle. Leaving £5 profit from each game!

Bike and Trailer Rides

Another popular St Peter's speciality!
With three playgrounds as well as a large school field we were able to dedicate one playground to bike and trailer rides. Parents with a bike and toddler trailer would bring it in to school and take turns to ride it around the playground offering riders to little ones. At 20p a lap, it was always very popular and needed nothing more than a bit of leg work!

Whack a Rat

Another handy dad! You just have to see the St Peter's wonderful whack a rat game on the successfulfundraisingforschools website!

We used to use a carpet roll tube for a drain pipe and a filled sock for the rat for this game. The idea is for people pay to try and whack the 'rat'. They hold a rounders bat or similar and the 'rat' is dropped in to the carpet tube which is hanging vertically. They then have to try and hit it as it comes out the bottom.

Charging around 20p a go makes it accessible for everyone. Offering a sweet to those who miss and something a little bigger for those who hit the rat worked well for us.

One summer a very clever dad made a brilliant stall with a real drainpipe and lots of decoration. He donated a toy rat and he and his son dressed up as rats to operate the stall. The difference this extra effort made to the takings was unbelievable. The whack a rat stall has proved one of the most popular at St Peter's fairs ever since and has been generously loaned to other schools and organisations to help them out too. It also made the press on several occasions!

Hair Braiding

Making a small charge for plaits, braids, ribbons and beads is another simple fundraiser for fairs. All you need is a few people who are good with hair.

Nail Painting

Nail painting is a simple and popular activity to introduce to fairs and fetes. At 20p or even 50p a go it can attract a lot of business. All you need is a team of willing volunteers to apply the nail varnish, much of which you are likely to obtain if you put out a request for donations of unwanted nail polish.

Welly Throwing

Welly throwing is more popular at summer fairs because it really does need to be an outside activity. It needs very little explanation; it is very simply a contest to see who can throw the wellington boot the furthest with a prize for the winner. You may want to split this in to age categories.

Candle Holders

A popular arts activity at any fair, but especially Christmas fairs, can be making tea light holders.

Put out a plea to parents for unwanted jam jars. Tie thin rope around the top for a handle and charge for people to use glass paint and pens to decorate them. They make ideal candle holders and lovely presents.

Grand Prix

One of our fair favourites was the Grand Prix. We would set up a Scalextric racetrack in a classroom and invite entrants at 20 or 30p a go. There would be races throughout the fair and the fastest time to complete the track would win a trophy, sponsored by one of the local garages.

We also tried this using Mario on a Wii and a PlayStation.

Remember you need to get any electrical equipment you use tested and certified before using it. Local qualified electricians will often do this for the school free of charge or you may find you have a suitably qualified parent at the school who can help.

Holiday Squares

We were lucky enough to have parents at school who owned holiday homes. They would donate a weekend or short break in one of their homes and we used it for a prize for holiday squares. Obviously you can use any prize for this, however you may be surprised how many people who own holiday homes will gladly provide a free weekend as it can be good advertising /publicity for them.

Just get a sheet of paper and draw up a large square containing 100 smaller squares numbered 1 to 100. People pay a fee – 50p or £1 - to have a go and put their name and telephone number in the numbered square they choose.

Before the end of the event a draw takes place 1-100 and the winning number wins the holiday or prize.

We found this event was supported by parents who couldn't attend the fair too. Volunteers successfully sold squares in the playground before and after school during the week prior to the event.

Coin in a Bucket

Another very simple idea. We would put a 20p coin in a bucket of water and people had to drop 10ps in and try and cover the 20p. This accumulated a lot of 10ps but if someone did cover the 20p, they either win the 20p or you have a selection of prizes for them to choose from.

Golden Envelopes

This was introduced by a long standing PTA member, who even after a serious illness and long after her children had left our school, continued to support our fairs by obtaining prizes for this activity.

You need a volunteer to write to as many local attractions as possible, from theme parks to zoos, play zones to sports centres, to ask for prizes.

Details of the prizes are put in golden envelopes numbered 1 to 12 which are then displayed on a big, eye catching board. For the Christmas fair we would market it as the 12 days of Christmas.

Cloakroom tickets are then folded and put in buckets and people pay 50p (the prizes are fantastic) a go. If they picked out a number 1 to 12 they won the corresponding prize. It is good to put in several numbers 1 to 12 and have some reserve envelopes ready so that the stall can continue throughout the event.

Warning! Don't put too many tickets in the buckets. The first time we ran this activity it was an hour before anyone won anything and in the last 10 minutes of the fair there were still six fantastic prizes remaining. People got a bit despondent so we learned from this and increased the chances of winning by increasing the number of winning tickets in the buckets and decreasing the non winning numbers.

Gift Wrapping

This activity is specifically for a Christmas fair.

Dedicate a classroom to provide a great opportunity for children to do their Christmas shopping cheaply and safely without a parent present.

Letters are sent home asking if they want their children to do their Christmas shopping at the fair. They fill in the form with their child's name and class and who they want presents for eg. mum, dad, granny and brother aged two. We always chose £3 per person but you can set whatever price you like.

The forms are returned to school with the money and each child is given a time slot.

The classroom is set up like a shop with tables displaying gifts for him and her, children's gifts etc. The gifts can be bought in under your budget, donated from local traders and businesses or they can be items taken from donations made by parents and friends in the run up to the fair.

You will also need plenty of wrap, scissors, sticky tape and a team of willing volunteers.

The room co-ordinator has the list of children they are expecting, who they are buying for and what time they are due to shop. The children turn up at the allotted time and choose the gifts they have already paid for. A volunteer then helps them wrap and label the presents and they leave with them all ready to go under the tree.

Throw a Sponge

An activity most suited to summer fairs!

Throwing a wet sponge at a teacher is a popular activity that children seem only too pleased to pay for! At St Peter's I don't think we ever managed to persuade a member of staff to have wet sponges thrown at them, however, there was always a long line of willing volunteers and I can honestly say we were never short of someone to take a soaking. Many schools hire in stocks for this activity or make their own 'set'.

Someone very kindly created a 'Sunshine Splash' for us, which came out year after year for our summer fairs and still does to this day. It is a wooden board with sunflowers painted on it and the centre of the sunflowers has been cut out so that people can put their faces in and await a soaking. The board protects the rest of the body from some of the water but not all it!

Sponges, buckets, water and somewhere for the victims to stand are all that are required. You will then need a couple of runners to refill buckets of water, volunteers to take a soaking and volunteers to take money and hand out three sponges to your paying customers.

Lollipop Tree

Another kind volunteer made us a wooden board in the shape of a Christmas tree with lots and lots of small holes drilled in to it. It was then painted green (obviously!!). We would stick small lollipops in the holes, some with a painted end to the stick which you can't see because it's the bit in the hole. We charged 20p a go. If the punters pulled out a stick with a red bit on the end they won a donated prize but if they didn't they walked away with the lollipop.

Lollipops can be bought for a few pence so the rest of the take is profit. If you don't want to use lollipops you can roll cloakroom tickets up and put them in the holes and operate the stall like a tombola.

Penalty Shoot Out

If you have goal posts at school you can easily organise a penalty shoot out. You need a couple of goal keepers and someone to take the money. People pay a small fee to take a turn – say 20p for six shots – and their score is recorded. Organise play offs half an hour before the end of the fair and keep going until there is an outright winner who wins the main prize. You can split the tournament in to different categories, perhaps age ranges, if you choose to, offering a prize for each categories.

Guess the name

Guess the name of a cuddly toy is another easy activity. Make a list of 25 or 50 names and charge people to guess which name is the correct name of the toy. Before you start put one of the names in a sealed envelope. Reveal the winning name as soon as all names have been sold.

You can do the same activity for guess the number of sweets in a jar or guess the weight of a cake.

MORE EVENTS AND ACTIVITIES

TOY SALE

A toy sale is an event that is most successful if you can involve the whole community, so publicising the event outside school is very important if you want to make the most of it. Blackboards, signs and posters around town to catch people's eye will complement your pre-arranged free newspaper coverage and school newsletters. Plan this event well in advance to maximise your publicity.

Our experience at St Peter's suggested that holding two toy sales a year works well. One in the spring and one in October or November so that parents can clear out their cupboards ahead of Christmas and also buy some Christmas bargains at the sale.

A toy sale involves you selling as new toys, games and play equipment for other people, usually at a half day sale held in the school hall. They get 75% of the amount charged and school gets 25%.

People are invited to drop off their quality unwanted items at school the afternoon before the sale and on the day of the sale, a few hours before the event begins. They must label each item with a tie on label detailing their name, contact number and the price of the item. They complete a form which lists and numbers all the items they want to sell. This is provided in duplicate (two copies). The corresponding number on the list for each item must also be entered on to the label which is attached to the goods. When sellers bring the items in, it is checked off on the seller's list to ensure everything is there. The seller takes away one copy of the list and you keep the other for reference at the sale. Examples of the forms can be found on and downloaded from the Successful Fundraising for Schools website. At this point each list should be stapled to an envelope, ideally C5 in size.

A two hour sale begins whereby customers pick up any toys they want to purchase from the goods displayed on tables around the room and take it to the check out gate. At the checkout volunteers cut the labels from the items and collect them in tubs. They calculate the total cost and take the money from the customers. It's handy to have a good supply of bags and boxes for people to use to carry their purchases home in and don't forget to organise a float so that you have plenty of change.

Another volunteer sorts all the labels from the sold goods and matches them up to the corresponding named envelopes to which the sellers' lists are attached. Each item on the list is ticked off as it is sold and the ticket from the sold item is placed inside the envelope as confirmation of the sale.

At the end of the sale the total for the items sold in each envelope is calculated using the attached list. 75% of the takings for each customer is put inside their envelope for collection. The seller is asked to produce his or her corresponding list at the collection point to identify themselves. They then sign to confirm receipt of the money handed to them before collecting unsold items.

An hour slot is given for collection of unsold good after the close of the sale. Unsold goods are sorted in piles around the room in alphabetical order. Sellers collect their envelope containing the money which is counted out in front of them before they sign for it. They then collect their unsold goods and take them away.

An option can be given to mark labels with a red cross meaning if the item is not sold it can be donated to school.

If you charge a small admission fee to the sale – say 50p for adults, children free – you are guaranteed an income even if nothing is sold!

Obviously the number of volunteers you need will depend on the size of your school and the size of your sale. I would suggest several checkers to receive goods in at each session and they can then help put the goods on display. When the event begins, two people will be needed to man the door, up to six to operate the checkout, two to sort tickets and four or five to total up sales and complete the sales envelopes. Two people will be needed to hand over the money and several more will be needed to help people recover their unsold items. It's useful to have a few more volunteers to help keep the displays looking good throughout the sale, to clear up at the end and also a couple of people to make the volunteers tea and coffee. Remember to have some reserves in case someone has to drop out last minute as this is one event where one man down can put a great deal of pressure on the rest of the team.

COFFEE MORNING

A coffee morning held in the school hall just after lessons start one morning is a great way for non-working parents to socialise and get to know each other. It can also provide an opportunity for childminders to get together. Turn the hall in to a mini café serving tea, coffee, cakes and biscuits. Organise some toys for pre-school children who may accompany their parent or carers. A raffle can boost funds too. This takes little planning and preparation, can last just an hour or so and raise well over £100 if you publicise it well enough.
This activity can also be organised an hour before school ends.

ICE CREAM TREATS

While this isn't something our school organised, many other PTAs I talked to found selling ice creams in the playground after school on Fridays a great way of raising funds. Moving the school freezer to outside a classroom window, where the power cable can be popped through the open window, allows the correct temperature for the ice creams to be maintained. A large tub of ice cream can fill dozens of small cones and it's something the children can look forward to at the end of each school week.

TRAY SALES

Ideal for Mother's and Father's Day.

The Mother's Day tray sale at our school was not only a good little earner, but it gave hundreds of children great pleasure. Each sale always raised more than £300 and there's not too much work involved. First of all you need to purchase enough polystyrene trays (similar to those some chip shops use) for every child in the school. It's great if you can find a local business to sponsor this event and purchase the trays for you.

On the Monday before Mothering Sunday you send a tray home with each pupil with a note asking them to fill it with goodies. This can be unwanted gifts, sweets, jewellery, toiletries etc. Ask everyone to return the trays to school on the Friday morning, presented as nicely as possible, preferably covered in cling film with a bow or ribbon added for decoration. Then at the end of school that day the children are invited to the Mother's Day sale in the school hall. The trays are sold for £1 each.

This event provides the pupils with the opportunity to buy their mum a gift for a reasonable sum and they can do their shopping in the safety of school premises. To bump up the profits and make it an enjoyable occasion for all, volunteers can set up a café area and serve teas, coffees and cakes to parents, carers and friends while the children are shopping.

Bric-a-brac and a raffle can also be introduced.

Just a word of warning - there is always a chance that some people won't return their trays or that some children will buy more than one, which could result in not enough trays to go round at the sale. To ensure no-one was disappointed we would usually plan ahead and a few volunteers grew daffodils in pots in time for the sale while others volunteered to fill some extra trays, just to make sure everyone had the opportunity to buy something.

You can always make some nice cup cakes with 'mum' iced on the top and put a clear wrap and bow on them for the children to buy as gifts too.

Recruiting year six pupils to help sell the items, accompanied by six or more adult volunteers worked for us.

The sale is complete within the hour, so this isn't a particularly time consuming event. It is however an extremely pleasurable experience for the pupils and ensures mum or dad get a nice gift for their special day without anyone spending a fortune.

AS NEW CLOTHING

There are a number of different ways to raise money from second hand clothes. One of these is covered in the section about recycling projects.

Asking parents to donate any school uniform that has been grown out of is a great way of helping other parents and make money for school.

At St Peter's we sold 'new to you' uniform for 50p per item. We organised stands at most school events but also regularly set it out in the playground before or after school or at school plays or parents evenings. We would leave an honesty box for people to put their 50ps in but if you have willing volunteers they can operate the stalls.

An 'as nu' clothing sale can also be organised in the same way the toy sale is organised. This can be an afterschool or weekend event where parents bring in all the labelled items they want to sell and the PTA sells them for 25% commission.

It's great to set up designer stalls and organising a fashion show to help sell the clothes can reap huge rewards. Alternatively, as new clothing stalls can be part of other school events like fairs, fetes and ladies pamper evenings.

FREE DONATIONS WHEN SHOPPING ONLINE

Parents, staff and friends of your school can create free donations for the school when they shop online, using their usual retailers.

There are a few websites that offer this service but one I have experience with is www.givingabit.com. Although it offers its service nationally, it is a family run business based in the town in which I live. If you have any queries or want some personal communication, you can contact the owner of the company using the contact form on their website.

Givingabit.com enables you to raise funds without any effort. The company does this by working with thousands of retail partners who have agreed to make a donation to a chosen cause every time a shopper clicks through to their site via givingabit.com and makes a purchase. The givingabit.com service is free as it is funded entirely by the retailers it works with. It does not cost you a penny to register your school and you could be raising money through your supporters' online shopping at no cost to them.

On average, 3% of the value of each purchase is donated to your school. For example, if you may make a purchase from Staples for £100, as a thank you, Staples will pay £3 to your school – at no cost to you. With so many shops signed up to the givingabit.com service, your school could benefit from everything from parents' and friends' weekly grocery shopping to their annual car insurance. The shops also provide givingabit.com with their latest discount codes, so your supporters could even save money whilst raising money.

Givingabit.com supplies you with free marketing resources to help you let your supporters know you are signed up to givingabit.com and the organisation prides itself on its customer service, helping you every step of the way. Knowing that volunteers on PTAs are very busy people, if you want a hand, givingabit.com will register your school for you. All you have to do is email contact@givingabit.com with your school details and they will do the rest.

100 CLUB

A 100 Club works by 100 members paying an annual amount of £12 by standing order (£1 a month). Prize draws are made monthly with a special draw at Christmas. You can set your own prize amounts but if you selected a first prize of £20, second prize of £10 and third prize of £5 the prize total would be £35 per month, leaving £65 a month for school funds. A special Christmas draw could see an increase in the prize fund for one week only. If you have enough willing participants the 100 Club can easily become a 200 club.

You need to be registered under the lotteries act to run this.

BONUS BALL LOTTO

If you don't have 100 people to run a 100 club, another idea is the weekly bonus ball lotto. You need 49 participants but can run it with fewer if need be.

Everyone who joins, signs up for the term or the year, whichever you choose. Each person is allocated a lottery number 1 to 49 and pays £1 a week to enter. Whoever holds the bonus ball number drawn on the day of your choice – say on Saturdays – wins £25. The remaining £24 goes in to school funds. £24 a week over a year is a good earner.

If you don't have 49 participants you can run it and adjust the winning amount. If a number is drawn for which there is no 'owner' the winnings also go in to school funds. This must be made quite clear to all those taking part before you start and you will need to have a lotteries licence in place.

FOREIGN CURRENCY

Why not ask people to donate any unwanted coins left over after their holiday overseas? Put a huge jar or bottle somewhere in school where donations can be made. www.cash4coins.co.uk is one of many ways to convert the coins to cash for school.

SCHOOL DISCO

The school disco is a great fundraiser and the children have a fabulous time. This is one event when the help of school staff, especially teachers and teaching assistants, is essential.
Because we had 400+ pupils we would run our after school discos in three sessions. The event invariably raised in excess of £500.

We booked a DJ from 3.30pm until 8pm. The reception class disco would run from 3.30pm-4.30pm. As the younger children left through one door, there would already be a queue forming at another door, of key stage one pupils whose disco ran from 4.45pm-6.15pm. The key stage two disco followed, running from 6.30pm until 8pm. We would usually all be on our way home by 8.30pm.

We sold tickets in the playground after school.

At the disco we served squash and crisps or biscuits which were included in the price and we gave everyone a chocolate bar to take home. The chocolate bars were usually sponsored by a local business. One Post is a local business that kindly supported us, despite it not being a business the general public would use and so not really directly benefitting from any publicity.

We used class lists when tickets were sold and ensured a contact number was written alongside the pupil's name. Volunteers ticked off each pupil as they arrived and staff helped the exit as they already knew the parents and could ensure children are taken home by the correct adult, just like they do at the end of a school day.

RACE NIGHT

A race night is a fantastic way to raise funds for your school but this is definitely an event for adults only and you will need a lotteries licence in place.

A race night involves your guests watching a series of horse or dog races on a big screen and betting on the runner they think will win. It can raise vast amounts of money through race sponsorship, a bar, betting and horse/dog ownership (our last race night thanks, to the Lions Club of Portishead and our co-ordinator Fiona, raised over £1,000.)

There are commercial organisations that will come in and run the whole event for you but this can cut your profits. You may also find that your local Lions Club or Rotary Club will be experienced in these events and will be happy to help organise yours, or you can just hire or buy a DVD with the races on and set up your own from scratch. Most school halls are equipped with a big screen and sound system these days, so it shouldn't be too difficult for novices to set up.

You will need some key people in place to begin with including a race night promotions manager who will put up posters, send out information in school newsletters, talk to local businesses to obtain prizes and sponsorship, put together a race night programme and sell them ahead of the event. You will also need a race night event manager who will reserve use of the school hall, organise the volunteers, ensure all the equipment is available and relevant licences are in place.

Ahead of the event invite sponsors for each race – this is a form of advertising for local businesses as their business features in the race night programme and gets several mentions from the MC during the evening. The sponsorship helps cover any costs of printing programmes and hiring race films and can add to the general profits of the evening.

Next you want owners for every horse in the programme – the owners name goes alongside or under the horse's name on the programme.

If you sell horses for £2 each, a race with 7 runners would give you £14, the owner of the winning horse for each race receives a bottle of wine. You may be able to get the wine donated as a prize from local shops or friends but if not, if you spend £4 on a bottle of wine, it's still an additional £10 profit from each race.

Programmes can be used as the race night tickets, they can be sold on the door or they can be given free of charge, this will depend on how you want to present your event. Some race nights charge £5 for a ticket which includes a ploughman's supper and a glass of wine. Others charge £2 for the programmes which are used to gain entry/act as tickets. You can decide on the combination that works best for you, taking in to consideration if you want to include catering in your evening.

During the event you will need a big personality master of ceremonies, tote ticket sellers to take the race night bets, tote ticket payout volunteers to pay the race winners and a projectionists/DVD operator to take care of the film and sound.

In addition to the key staff you will need support volunteers to generally help set up, act as doormen, take care of the bar and catering, sell race night programmes, raffle tickets and clean up afterwards.

You will need to decide on the size of each race night bet, we always stuck to 50p, and you need to decide what percentage of the race night tote will go to the school. The remainder is what is used for the payout.

Once you have welcomed everyone you need to open the race night tote for the first race. Punters may place as many bets on as many horses as they wish in the race you are about to show. It is important to make sure that betting is handled efficiently. You will need four volunteers seated at a table to sell Tote tickets on each race. Each ticket seller can handle tickets for two horses. When all bets have been placed the race night tote must be closed, this is to comply with current legislation. Once the race night tote is closed the race is selected by an audience member and shown.

A separate pay-out point should be set up for the winning horse. While the race is on, your pay-out volunteers calculate the winnings. They add up the total funds taken, take out the percentage you have chosen for school and the remainder is divided equally between those who bet on the winning horse (round up or down to the nearest 10p). As soon as the race is over, the pay-out dividend is announced and the lucky punters collect their winnings from the pay-out point. This is repeated for the six or eight races you have chosen, breaking in the middle for refreshments and raffle. Also allow 10-20 minutes between each race for use of the bar, conversation and study of the race programme.

There are lots of ways to end the evening, you can just close after the final race or you can add a prize draw or auction to round off the event.

SPONSORED EVENTS

Sponsored events come in all shapes and sizes and most children love a challenge. Sponsored activities can pull in much needed funds without too much preparation, but don't take it for granted that just because pupils at your school are asked to take part in a sponsored walk they will all bring in pots of money when it is complete. They need to be excited by the challenge you set them. Engage with teaching staff and ask for their support. Get the children's interest by introducing a theme. Come up with a realistic target and perhaps offer a treat if this is exceeded. Let the pupils know how important it is to raise the funds and how they will benefit from them.

Refreshments afterwards can be another nice touch and a computer printed certificate to congratulate them all on their efforts is always appreciated.

If the event takes place in school time you will have to clear it with the head teacher and staff. Staggering the times pupils take part might be useful if it is something involving the whole school. A sponsored walk can take place throughout the day with different year groups starting every hour. Reception children are likely to be given a smaller distance to walk than year six pupils. Perhaps younger children should be asked to complete laps of the playground while older children walk around the school field. You can inject more fun by introducing a song or chant to march to.

You will need marshals for the event and all pupils will need a full information sheet and a sponsored form to take home.

Don't forget to let your local newspaper know the event is happening so that they can send a photographer along at the end to capture everyone celebrating their success.

The list of sponsored activities is endless but some suggestions are listed below to be going on with. You can also involve friends of the school, school governors and local businesses.

Some larger businesses do match funding for charities, especially if one of their employees is involved, so it's worth asking parents if their employers have such schemes.

Sponsored events can include: walk, spelling, bouncing (on a bouncy castle which you can hire in), litter picking, swimming, dancing, silence, read-a-thon, car wash, weeding, knitting, singing….. there are many more, so just put your thinking caps on.

CAKE SALES

An after school cake sale at our school, organised by a specific year group, raised anything between £80 and £300. We asked every year group to organise one cake sale during the school year. A volunteer parent in each year group is appointed to co-ordinate their year's event. A note is sent home asking parents to bake cakes and biscuits and send them in to school in a labelled, airtight container on the day of the sale. At the end of school a couple of tables are set up in the playground and fairy cakes, cup cakes and muffins are sold by volunteers and pupils for 40p each. A great end to the school day!

This is purely optional but we would always ensure the amount each sale raised was spent on items for the year group that organised it.

CHRISTMAS SHOPPING EVENING

November is a great time to organise an adult only Christmas shopping event. Invite local businesses, art and craft organisations and individuals to take trade stands at your event for a set fee.
When setting the fee make sure it is relevant to the amount of people you are expecting to attend, it needs to be worthwhile for the businesses to come along. St Peter's usually charged £15 per stand which made it appealing to even the smallest of businesses.

The idea of the Christmas Shopping evening is to make buying Christmas gifts a pleasurable experience as the festive season approaches, without the hustle and bustle of mall shopping.
You can charge a small entry fee and invite customers to purchase some of their Christmas gifts from the array of stalls. Then if you set up a gift wrapping area, you can charge a small fee to wrap the gifts, while the customers enjoy a glass of wine and some snacks in the bar area you have set up. After an hour relaxing and socialising with friends, the shoppers pick up their gifts all ready to go under the tree.

You can add to this a fashion show, some entertainment or other suitable activities, but remember to keep it focussed around the shopping event.

Don't forget to apply for a licence if selling alcohol.

GREETINGS CARDS

Children can have their drawings professionally reproduced on to high quality greetings cards which can be sold to parents and carers to help raise funds for school. We tried several companies offering this facility and eventually stuck with Cauliflower Cards which offered us a good deal and great customer service.

School Christmas Cards Project

We have used Cauliflower Cards for many years; it is one of the biggest school Christmas card printing companies in the UK. Established in 2006, Erika Speirs an experienced primary school teacher and her husband Hugh, who had already established a successful printing company, had a wealth of knowledge, enthusiasm and  experience between them to launch an exciting range of fundraising projects specifically aimed at primary schools. The company has grown successfully over the years but still prides itself on providing the personal touch and will always go the extra mile to meet customer needs.

School Christmas Cards are Fantastic for School Fundraising

The School Christmas Card Project is a fantastic fundraising activity for schools and very popular amongst parents, grandparents, and family friends who love to send and receive something with a more personal touch. Parents are always keen to support this activity as they would be buying Christmas cards anyway - and of course these ones will be special!

Encouraging Creativity - Boosting Pupils Self Esteem

Cauliflower Cards allows the use of a wide range of art materials so that children can really enjoy producing the artwork. Children love the process of creating their designs and school feedback has confirmed real excitement when the children see their cards professionally printed and beautifully packaged.

Everyone can be involved

Cauliflower Cards has a wide range of greetings that can be selected to print inside the cards. Greetings include: Eid, Diwali, Thank You, a range of Christmas greetings including Welsh and Gaelic, Seasonal Greetings or alternatively cards can be left blank inside to allow for any other uses.

The Cards

The Christmas Card Project works by producing professional packs of cards from each child's original artwork. The cards have the child's name as the designer on the back, along with a fundraising message where schools/PTA's can specify what the fundraising will be for (this could be a general message for example the school name or could specify a particular project).

The Fundraising

The schools take orders for the packs of cards and retain a proportion of the order money as their fundraiser. The more packs sold the more money the school will raise. This is an extremely good method of fundraising as most families send Christmas cards and parents are happy to purchase special personalised cards that can be sent out to family and friends. You can even include a family photo or photos of the children on the cards, which is something I have done in the past, as an extra as well as my children creating their own cards.

Taking Part in the Project

When a school registers online at www.cauliflowercards.co.uk to take part in the Christmas Card Project they receive all the materials they need to run the project. This will include: order forms for every child incorporating an A4 sheet for their design, administrative materials, a free return courier sack and colourful printed posters along with sample cards to help promote Christmas card sales. The Cauliflower Cards website also has useful sections for promoting sales and running the project and a fantastic gallery of designs to help with design ideas. Once orders have been collected a courier will be organised by Cauliflower Cards to collect the artwork. The cards will be delivered back to school by the first week of December.

Testimonials

St Peter's Primary is one of many schools to benefit from Cauliflower Cards. Here are more testimonials.

"Firstly a huge thank-you from our committee and our school for the fantastic turnaround with the Christmas Cards. It's our third year using you and we were really happy with the whole service and also the profits we made."
PTA Member, Great Chesterford Primary School

"Thank you so much for the cards, they were returned so quickly! Everyone was really pleased. We would definitely like to take part again next year. Very impressed with the quality of the cards."
PTA Chair Frances Olive Anderson Lea School

www.cauliflowercards.co.uk Tel: 0800 043 2273

FUN MATS

Here is another great way to raise funds making use of your school's greatest asset – your pupils' creativity.

Art based fundraising projects, as mentioned previously with the cards, provide an opportunity for children to create imaginative drawings that can then be used to make a variety of quality products that have tremendous parent appeal.

These projects can be fun and also very rewarding. Children enjoy creating their drawings and get very excited when they see them featured on real products and schools can easily incorporate creating the artwork into normal school activities. In addition parents are able to buy useful items featuring their child's drawing either as keepsakes for themselves or as gifts for family members.

In my experience, the more profitable and rewarding projects create products from individual children's drawings rather than collective artwork or pictures selected as the best of a group. It is seeing their own child's drawing featured on a number of quality products that encourages parents to buy and helps schools to raise funds.

There are a number of artwork-based fundraising projects available and one of my favourites is FunMats. The FunMats project offers 10 attractive, quality products, each featuring an individual child's artwork, produced from one single drawing. The products include coasters, computer mouse mats, shopping bags, place mats, framed prints, t-shirts and more. Parents are able to purchase any quantity of as many products as they wish. There is no minimum order, either in terms of participating children or in the products on offer to parents.

Schools are supplied with booklets comprising the drawing paper and a parent's order form together with drawing guidelines and promotional materials showing the range of products available to parents.

A key benefit of the FunMats project is that it is cash positive and risk free. Nothing is paid out until payment for the orders has been collected from parents and the profit banked. There are no charges for unsold products or for carriage. It even costs nothing to call FunMats on a Freephone 0800 number.

As schools make a profit without incurring any initial costs this enables new PTAs, with no cash resources, to kick-start their fundraising campaign. No school, nursery, club or group is too small or too distant, to undertake a FunMats project. The company helps small brownie packs, crèches, after-school clubs and playgroups to raise funds and there are schools that regularly undertake the FunMats project as far afield as the Shetland Isles and the Channel Islands.

Whilst most schools raise funds for their own needs such as teaching aids and equipment that local authorities are unable to fund, some undertake the FunMats project to raise funds for charities. Again the risk free element of the project makes this a very safe option.

The company is very customer focussed and user friendly with very clear information and guidance for teachers and PTA members running the project. In the event of queries or problems, a call on the Freephone number, during office hours, will connect to helpful people. Real people!

FunMats, which has been operating for eighteen years, is one of the leading providers in the UK of art-based school fundraising products and helps approximately 600 schools, nurseries and youth groups to raise funds each year.

The company is based in Malvern, Worcestershire, where all the product development and manufacturing are carried out using ethically sourced materials.

The recently updated FunMats [www.funmats.co.uk] website is well worth a visit.

CALENDARS

Allowing the pupils to help create a school calendar is great fun. They make wonderful Christmas presents too, so if you get the price right they can prove very popular and be a winner when it comes to fundraising.

There are different ways to produce calendars and with the committees I have worked with, we have tried just about all of them. There have been positives and negatives in all cases, so you really need to choose what suits you and your school best.

Basically the calendar is produced on A4 paper or card, or A3 folded to A4. It hangs like this:

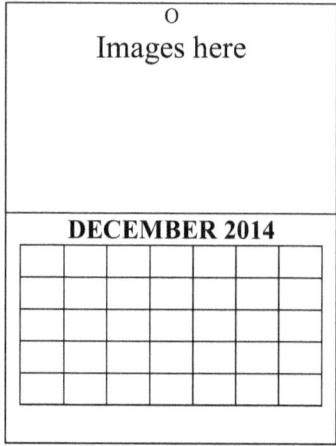

Pupils draw a head and shoulders picture of themselves and stick it on the images section of the month in which their birthday occurs. The individual names can then be written or printed under each drawing.

In the early days we used to get the children to create pen and ink drawings. That way it was all in black and white, allowing us to photocopy each sheet fairly cheaply and use the comb binding machine in school to bind the pages for each calendar. A team of volunteers made them and we sold them for around £2. It was nearly all profit and because they were so cheap almost all parents at school bought at least one. These days that model might seem a bit dated.

It's worth putting a request in the school newsletter to ask for any parents who work in the printing trade to come forward. It still takes a number of volunteers to do the prep, but with someone working 'in the know', a more professional finish can be achieved and you would almost certainly be able to produce them in colour. If they look more professional you can charge more, but they may also cost you more to produce.

There are online packages to help you create your own calendars or of course there are professional companies that specialise in creating calendars for schools. They provide you with all you need to know and a kit that makes putting the whole thing together extremely simple. They offer many different formats from which you can choose your design. They charge you a fixed amount per calendar and you add on the amount of profit you choose.

I strongly suggest asking parents and friends to pre-order calendars before you print, as you can never be sure of how many you will sell. We have had years when we have sold out in a couple of days and others where we have limped in to February still trying to sell the calendars we have left. We have even ended up offering them as prizes somewhere along the lines!

SCHOOL OR PTA MAGAZINE

If you already issue a regular PTA newsletter to parents and staff, adding paid for advertisements from local businesses could help you develop it in to a monthly magazine which not only pays for itself but brings in additional revenue.

With most people having access to desktop publishing this isn't a difficult task. You may even be able to involve pupils by running an after school or lunch time magazine club.

FAMILY DISCO/BARBECUE

A family disco or barbecue is an opportunity to get lots of families and friends together and raise money for your school. It is very simple to organise and can involve as much or as little as you choose.

Work out how much you want to make from the event, calculate your costs and set your ticket prices accordingly. We usually go for something like £3 for adults, children go free or £2.50 for adults, £1 for children or £6 for a family ticket. Don't make it too expensive as this might exclude some families. The more people you sell tickets to the better the atmosphere and more you will take on the food, drinks and raffle.

If you are going to have a licensed bar you will need to make it clear that no children are admitted without adults and ensure your bar volunteers are clear on the rules about selling alcohol. Make sure there are plenty of soft drinks available and perhaps introduce a non alcoholic cocktail bar too.

To begin with book the school hall and of course you will need a disco. It's always a good idea to ask if any parents run a disco before looking further afield.

For many years we used a disco that included art and craft activities. The event would begin at 6.30pm when a large tarpaulin was placed across the floor and art and craft activities would be spread out. For one hour the children would make pirate hats, tissue paper covered parrots or posters and flags, while music played quietly in the background. This gave the adults a chance to chat while the children used their creative skills. Then at 7.30pm the tarpaulin was rolled up and put away and the disco began.

If you are going to organise a barbecue, burgers and sausages go down well, include a vegetarian option and a few bowls of salad and you're done!

Don't forget that a raffle, silent auction or a stall or two can boost funds too.

MONEY MAKING LABELS

All schools ask parents to label clothing carefully so that if items get lost they can be returned to their rightful owner. This is an important part of school life which becomes even more important if it can raise funds for your school.

We used Easy2name which operates a very successful fundraising scheme. Any orders the company receives from parents at your school, by post, phone or online at www.easy2name.com, raises 20% commission for your cause.

Starting up is simple, you just register your school with Easy2name for free and they will send you a fundraising pack. This includes:
Order forms (as many as you need)
Stickers with the school name on (to identify the forms)
Samples
Posters

All you need to do is stick the labels on to the order forms and distribute them to parents, usually by sending them home in book bags. New parents evenings are also a great time to promote the labels. The parents place their orders directly with Easy2name and the organisation sends the labels straight back to the customers, so as a PTA you have no work to do other than distributing the order forms and promoting labels, reminding parents that by ordering the labels in this way, they are helping to raise funds for the school.

After registering, as a PTA you are able to log in at www.easy2name.com at any time to view your total sales and the commission you have raised. You can then claim the money as often as you like and funds are paid directly into the group's bank account.

Schools can raise more than £300 a year in this way, increasing sales by remembering to mention the scheme in newsletters and by including a link to the Easy2name website. Another benefit of course is reducing the dreaded lost property pile!

To sign up or find out more visit
www.easy2name.com/login-fundraising.htm or call 01635 298326

RECIPE BOOK

Everyone has great recipes to share and what better way to raise funds for school than inviting pupils and their families to help create a recipe book?

You may decide to include as many contributions as possible, combine children's artwork with parents' recipes or run a competition to find the best recipes to publish.

If you want something different you could ask members of staff for their favourite recipes or produce a book based on school meals.

Obtaining a sponsor for each recipe will boost funds even more.

With a quick online search you will find plenty of organisations all set up ready to help you produce a recipe book which you can sell to make a profit. Alternatively your local print shop or parents working in the print industry may be able to help you produce your own book. Desk top publishing packages prove very useful for this kind of thing too. This may involve a little more work on your part, but could increase the profits.

REWARD SCHEMES

Ask local companies if they would be interested in starting a reward or loyalty scheme. They agree to make a donation to school related to the amount of sales they make to parents and friends of the school. Eg. An estate agent may offer to pay £100 to the school if it sells a property for a parent, or the local shoe shop may stamp a card every time a parent or supporter of the school buys a pair of shoes and for every six or 10 stamps it donates £5 to the school. A garden centre may want to advertise its Christmas trees through the school and in return donate back 10% of all purchases made through the school. The list is endless.

EASTER BINGO

You can organise a bingo game at any time of the year. We often chose Easter because it's a great time for a family occasion and also because we found it relatively easy to find a sponsor for Easter eggs as prizes.

A local business, in our case, usually Heritage estate agents, handing over £100 worth of Easter eggs provides a great photo opportunity for the local press and some much appreciated free publicity for the business. We sometimes however, alternated the annual event at this time of year with the school disco, because that too can benefit from the sponsorship of several boxes of small Easter eggs used as a take home gift for pupils.

So, back to Easter bingo.....
We would organise this in the school hall on the last Saturday morning of term before Easter, although we also tried it after school on the last Friday of term. Obviously, you can hold it whenever it suits you.

Little preparation is needed before the day. Advertise the event in the school newsletter and you will need to find a sponsor to deliver the prizes you need to school. You will also need some bingo books donated by your local stationer, a one hundred square for the caller's number board, numbers1-99 on small squares of card, an overhead projector (OHP), some blank acetates, ideally a microphone and some school pencils.

The number square can be used on the OHP with a different acetate for each game which allows you to mark the numbers as they are called and at the end of each game, remove the used acetate and replace it with a fresh one.

If you want to add a really nice touch, you can add a final 'bonus' game. You make the final bingo game card yourself using exactly the same numbers, but placed randomly on the card in different orders, so that nobody notices they all have the same number. This game is for the children only. You will need a special set of numbers for the caller for this last game so that the game doesn't go on too long. No-one realises that everyone is a winner and it is very amusing when everyone in the room calls house at the same time. The prize for the last game is just a mini egg from a big basket, but everyone goes home a winner.

Chairs should be set out in rows facing the screen in the hall and the Easter egg prizes should be displayed on a table. A caller's table is set out at the front with the OHP, acetates and numbers.

You will need volunteers to sell bingo books, call the numbers, check the numbers of the winning games and to hand out prizes.

To boost funds it is a good idea to have volunteers selling refreshments and raffle tickets for an egg prize.

We charged no admission fee but sold two books and the bonus game card to each participant for £2. Everyone can play as the prizes are Easter eggs not cash, but children should be accompanied by an adult.

Once books have been bought and everyone is seated welcome them to the event and explain the rules. Explain they cross off the numbers in their books for the game being played as they are called. If you decide the winner will be the first person to complete a line in the first game, which is on the red page, then explain that and then show everyone the prize they are playing for. The first to call bingo or house is the winner but their numbers should be checked before handing over the prize. Then you move on to the next game. You can play for a line, for four corners or for a full house.

Stop for a break half way through to draw the raffle, enjoy the refreshments and even allow people to browse stalls if you decided to introduce them.

The whole event is usually through in two hours and can easily raise at least couple of hundred pounds.

TEA TOWELS

Fundraising tea towels can be used for any occasion: Christmas, Easter, Mother's Day, end of term etc.

A variety of organisations offering a simple process to help you create a school or class tea towel can be found online. My research suggests that you can purchase the final product for between £1.35 and £2, depending on the quantity your order. Then you add on what you see fit to be the profit you make on each item and you have your final sale price.

The tea towels can feature pictures drawn by pupils of themselves or of the staff, with a wide choice of borders to suit the occasion. Alternatively if you have a special event or anniversary to mark, an image of the school building or relevant item can be included.

The tea towels can be sold via order forms sent home in book bags or via Parent Mail. They can also be sold at school events, parents' evening or in the playground after school.

RECYCLING PROJECTS

There are numerous recycling projects that can help your school raise funds. Use a search engine to see what is around as many of them are regionalised. From clothes to ink cartridge recycling, many companies will collect your used goods and pay you handsomely for them.

We use Bristol Textile Recyclers (BTR). The organisation collects unwanted textiles: clothes, curtains, sheets etc. and after washing them, sends many of them to developing countries overseas to be used. They pay a certain amount per ton for the clothes to your school or charity. They arrange a collection time, send you confirmation of the weight they collected and then put the coffers in your bank account. It couldn't be easier! All you have to do is ask parents to bring their unwanted items to school on the morning of the collection. BTR issues sacks for the clothes and letters to send home but the textiles can just be put in to carrier bags or bin lines too.

CAR BOOT SALE

Car boot sales make great fundraisers and can help you get rid of unwanted items at the same time! The key to a successful car boot sale is good advertising. Posters, leaflets and plenty of notice in local papers are all a must.

Ideally hold the sale in the school car park, playground or field but if those are out of the question find an alternative site in a visible location. If you are raising money for school a business owner may be willing to allow you to use his car park free of charge for your sale. If you do this, don't forget to check with your local council for restrictions or permits.

Choose the date and location, set a fee for cars, say £5 each and start taking bookings. My experience suggests that most people like to turn up without booking, so be prepared for queues when you open up. Have someone on hand to guide the cars and tell them where to park up and make sure someone is around to help them exit at the end too.

It's always good to decide what will happen in case of rain and explain this on your publicity material. Let people know that it will be cancelled if there is heavy rain and a new date will be arranged, or if you are going to go ahead no matter what the weather, let people know and make it clear whether refunds will be made or not for people who don't want to go ahead in the rain.

TABLE TOP SALE

A table top sale works using the same principles as the car boot sale. The only difference is that you hold it inside. The upside is that you are not affected by the weather but the down side is that space is more restricted.

The table top sale, just like a car boot sale can operate by selling pitches to people who want to sell their second hand items. An alternative is to organise a table top sales just for small businesses to operate from which includes cottage industries, artists etc.

TREASURE HUNT

A treasure hunt can be a great fundraising activity for both children and adults.

For a children's treasure hunt it's best to keep it to a confined space, the school grounds or school building are ideal. However if you are organising a family treasure hunt, it can be set over a wider area and include landmarks in your home town or village. Teams pay a fee to enter and donated items are given as prizes. You can award prizes for the person to solve the most clues, the first person to finish and claim the treasure chest and for the best team name. If you are opening the treasure hunt up to the whole community you can split teams up in to categories if you have enough prizes.

A great deal of preparation is required. You will need treasure hunt sheets for each team containing clues to different destinations and a list of questions that can only be answered if the participant has arrived at the right spot.

You will need some marshals along the route to ensure that no-one gets lost. It's a good idea to get mobile telephone numbers of those taking part and give a contact number of the hunt co-ordinator so that the organisers can be contacted during the hunt and you can contact anyone who fails to turn up at the end.

Set a time limit for the hunt and arrange for everyone to meet back at school to claim their prize and hand in their answers. This is also a good opportunity to raise more funds. The prize giving ceremony can include the sale of food and drink, stalls and raffles. If you make this an annual event and have a perpetual trophy to hand on each year, it can create some ongoing friendly rivalry.

QUIZ NIGHT

Organising a quiz night to raise funds is not that hard, providing you sit down and plan it properly. Preparation will be the key to the success of the actual night.

We always made our quiz nights for adults only and these have raised between £250 and £560. However there is nothing to stop you organising a family quiz night, or even a children's quiz night. Obviously no alcohol if it's a junior quiz.

Some years we held our annual quiz at an outside venue. Holding the event outside school definitely attracts more staff teams. If we held it at the local social club, no preparation of the venue was required, we didn't need to obtain an alcohol licence and we didn't need to organise a bar and buy in refreshments to sell. However the main advantage of holding the quiz at school means you get the profits on the refreshments which can make a huge difference to the proceeds of the evening.

Decide on a date for your quiz and work out how much money you would like to make from the event. Set your team entry fee and then do your sums to work out how many people you need to attend to make the money you want to make. So if you want to make a minimum of £250 from your quiz night and you charge £10 for a team of four people (£2.50 per person), you know that you need 25 teams to enter. Entry money alone will then bring you

£250. Deduct any expenses and rest assured that if you get your 25 teams you know what your bottom line profit will be.

Recruit someone to ask local shops and businesses for raffle prizes as a raffle on the night will bump up your profits.

On top of this, if you are running your own bar and refreshments, you will need to buy the goods in to sell and organise volunteers to serve them. Work out what profit you want to make on your refreshments and make a price list accordingly.

If you are running your own bar, don't leave it too late to apply to the local council for your alcohol licence.

So, you choose the venue, set your prices, organise your bar and raffle (don't forget to purchase raffle tickets), next you need a quiz master. A big personality makes it more fun, especially someone with a good sense of humour. Your quiz master sets the questions – say between five and 10 rounds of 10 questions – keeping a good mix of subjects. A quiz can be a disaster if no-one can answer any of the questions, but it can be just as disastrous to ask questions that absolutely everyone can answer. Think of your target audience when setting the questions. Your quiz master will need a PA system to make sure he can be heard. You will also need some volunteer markers to check the answer sheets after each round.

See if a local business will sponsor a trophy for the winner and some bottles of wine for the teams coming second and third.

Think about how you will publicise your charity quiz night. Nobody will turn up for it if they don't know about it. The school newsletter is a good start and perhaps some staff and parent lobbying. Ask your local papers to include it in their 'What's On' section and put up posters around town to attract attention.

All you have left to do then is enjoy it!

DINNER DANCE

The first dinner dance I ever helped organised was one of the scariest events I have ever helped put together when it comes to balancing the books. It's the only time I have ever entered in to an event with a possible £100 loss hanging over my head. Fortunately the evening ended with a profit of £2,000 and the dinner dance became a popular fundraiser for many years.

If you feel you may struggle to sell sufficient tickets to make the evening a success, holding it in November or December allows you to invite local businesses to join you and use it as their Christmas party.

First you need to choose your date and venue. We always hired a large hall in the centre of town that has its own bar and kitchen, but you could hold it at school, organising your own bar, or you may want to use a local hotel, pub or club with its own in-house facilities.

If you need to use outside caterers have a chat to several different ones and see if you can speak to people who have used their services before deciding which company to choose.

You will need to select your menu giving guests a choice and don't forget to include a vegetarian option.

Choose your table size, we would usually go for tables of 10 or 12 but make it clear in your publicity that smaller groups of people can buy tickets and join another party.

Once the caterers have been booked, you will need to organise the drinks and the evening's entertainment.

You could also do with a team of volunteers to secure plenty of donated raffle and auction prizes.

If you can involve some local businesses you may be able to arrange a goody bag for each guest to take home with them.

Robert John, a hairdressing group local to our school, was always very willing to supply bags for our guests to take home which promoted their services and provided guest with lots of wonderful free product samples.

Another favourite is to ask cafes, restaurants, pubs and sports clubs to donate a free drink, meal, fitness class etc. Tape an envelope under guests' chairs, each with one of these prizes in. Then put a pot on each table and during the evening ask everyone to donate £1 in order to trigger a surprise. Once a pot has been collected from each table with the correct amount of money in, ask the guests to look under their chairs and reveal their prizes. Great fun!

It's a good idea to put together a display somewhere in the hall showing how the money raised from the event will be spent.

Once you have booked everything you need, make sure you get your sums right. Total up the costs, work out how many people your event can accommodate or how many it is realistically likely to attract and set your ticket price accordingly.

You will need to provide a menu with the publicity material being distributed and a booking form. Ask for a non-refundable deposit to be made upon booking.

The auction, silent auction and raffle can be big fund boosters for this event.

On the day of the event:

Decorating the room will help create the atmosphere.
Make sure someone is at the door to welcome your guests. Direct them to the cloakroom, to the display showing details of what the money raised will be used for and to the silent auction display where they can make sealed bids.

You will need an MC to ensure the evening flows, to introduce the various activities and host the auction. If you have a celebrity in town who will run the auction for you in return for a free dinner, all-the better! The bigger the personality of the MC, the better the atmosphere and the MC can also keep everyone focussed on what the evening is about – raising funds for that special project.

We have used a table magician to welcome people and keep them entertained whilst everyone is arriving.

A comedian can be a great ice breaker getting the evening off to a flying start; but it can also get it off to a bad start if you choose the wrong act so do some research before you make your booking.

Once people are relaxed you can send your raffle ticket sellers off to their job.

Soft background music is ideal while the meal is eaten and then after the meal, especially once the wine is flowing, a grand auction can raise hundreds, if not thousands of pounds.

Dancing to a live band or a disco for the last two hours can round the evening off nicely.

AUCTION OF PROMISES

An auction of promises doesn't have to cost anything to run. From an hour's gardening to an introductory French lesson, an auction of volunteered services is a fantastic way of raising money.

This can be run as an after school event over a cup of coffee or as a big social event with a bar and maybe a barbecue or music.

The first things to do, is organise some promises for the auction. Send a form home with each pupil asking parents to consider what skills or services they could donate. Head up the form I am giving...' with room for a description of the promise. Ask the giver to include how much the donation is worth and any conditions attached to it. Make sure the name, address and telephone number of the giver are included so that the person with the winning bid can claim their prize.

Next, cast the net in to the wider community to see if businesses, councillors, local celebrities and your local MP will make a contribution. This should all be done well in advance of the event, say 3-4 weeks before.

Ideas for donations can vary considerably.
Here are some ideas of what you might expect:
- Ironing services
- Babysitting
- Dog walking
- Car wash
- A free car MOT
- A blow dry at the local salon
- Sports coaching
- Dinner for two at a local restaurant
- Gardening

A week or so before the auction make sure you get plenty of publicity. Number each lot and publish the list, sending it out to all parents, friends and carers with an invitation to attend. To add a bit of fun you could have one or two secret lots. Also provide a facility for people who cannot attend to submit postal bids.
Make sure people know when and how they will need to pay.
Mention some of the most unusual or exciting donations in the local media and put posters up wherever you can.

Next you need to elect an auctioneer - someone with a big personality who can make amusing quips, but who can also handle the crowd. They will need to call out the item on offer, with a brief description and what it's worth and then start the bidding. You will need several volunteer runners to collect the details of the highest bidder and take the money.

A good PA system is vital because if the auctioneer cannot be heard clearly, people won't bid.

Put out tables and chairs for the event. Make sure everyone is welcomed upon arrival, knows what to do and feels comfortable and relaxed. Enjoy the event and take as much money as you can!

FASHION SHOW

If you are looking for a fundraising event that combines entertainment and glamour, a fashion show could be the answer.

If you are going to organise this from scratch you will need to start planning at least six months before the event. However there are organisation that will do everything for you and all you have to do is book them and sell tickets!

Let's look at organising one from scratch.
The school hall or drama studio is the ideal venue. You will also need fashions and accessories. These can come from designers and manufacturers or if you are going to hold an as new fashion show, you need to find sellers of quality garments and items. You will also need models and entertainers.

Six key personnel will help you make your event a success; these are a show producer, backstage manager, publicist, model co-ordinator, sponsor and clothing liaison officer and sales manager.

The show producer creates the budget, chooses the theme and organises all the personnel required. The backstage manager oversees the production of the show, the publicist generates publicity for the event and the model co-ordinator organises volunteer models and co-ordinates fittings, they can also recruit volunteer hairdressers and make-up artists. The sponsor and liaison person sources designers and manufacturers to provide products, some donated and some sold on a commission basis. The sales manager is responsible for tickets sales, corporate sponsorship and any other potential income activities.

Make sure you have a good sound system and lighting for the event. A good compare will make a big difference to the success of the event. Produce a programme and sell advertising space to pay for the printing and generate profit. Include some light entertainment to begin the event and in the middle. Hold a raffle that is drawn at the end of the show, before guests start trying on clothes.

Put up posters, send out a newsletter, sell your tickets, invite VIPs and create a buzz. Invite journalists and fashion writers, staff and governors. Send out press releases including relevant photos of models wearing the costumes that will be on sale, maybe also with one or two of the organisers or the benefactors.

Organise refreshments and make sure you apply for a licence if you want to serve alcohol.

TALENT SHOW

Talent shows can be a lot of fun, but they can also be a lot of hard work. With good organisation you can present a fundraising talent show that will knock the socks off your audience.

Whether you go for an adult talent show, a children's talent show or a combination of both, these events can reveal some hidden skills and talents that surprise an audience, providing a wonderful evening of entertainment.

Once you have held one talent show, it is likely the school will want one every year!

You will need plenty of lead time for this event so start planning months in advance.

Decide what age ranges you want in your show. I'm going to suggest a combination of adults and children, not just the age of children in your school but maybe include their siblings too, so that it s a real community affair.

Start by asking for people to nominate acts or for people to sign themselves up. Use a basic application form to explain what talent they would like to present in the show. Encourage a mix of parents, teachers, grandparents, boys, girls, teenagers etc.

Decide how many acts you can include, presenting 10-15 minute slots. If you are having a 2 ½ hour show with a 30 minute interval, eight acts would be ideal. However if you have lots of interest and you don't want to disappoint, you could run five minute acts or a combination.

Once you have lots of application forms, hold auditions and get a board of judges to help you decide who goes through to the show. Include as much variety as you can and make sure you have some reserves who will step in if people cancel or are ill on the day.

When you have your acts, you are ready to prepare for the show. Book the hall, organise your lighting and sound system, set your ticket price and print your tickets, produce a programme, engage a host or MC, organise a bar and refreshments and don't forget the ever important raffle.

Give your artists a good month to perfect their act while you let the community know the show is taking place. Flyers, newsletters and perhaps a story in the local press are all ways to generate interest.

At least a week prior to the show, organise some rehearsals, to run exactly as you want the show to run. Choose your host carefully as the stronger the host you have the smoother the show appears. Hold a technical rehearsal first, ensuring you have all the equipment and props required by each act. Keep a running list of each requirement which will be essential for your back stage volunteers. They will need to help each act enter the stage in order, set the microphones for each and make sure props are accessible.

Open 'big' and finish 'big', so choose your strongest acts for first and last. Also come up with some kind of finale. Keep variety in place to hold the interest of the audience, mixing up the acts so you don't have four dancers in a row.

Sell your tickets in advance, ensure everyone knows what they are doing and enjoy the show. Mistakes may happen but it's all good fun in the name of fundraising.

PAMPER EVENINGS

Pamper evenings tend to be one for the ladies but they don't have to exclude men. In fact we have used these evenings to raise more money by persuading male teachers to take part in a sponsored leg wax.

Ladies pamper evenings give women a chance to relax and enjoy shopping opportunities in an informal environment, while taking advantage of health and beauty treatments, therapies and the odd glass of wine!

Beauty services and holistic therapies are often the type of businesses run by mums with school aged children. Qualified therapists often choose to go 'mobile' when they have children so they can work during hours to suit their families.

So first things first - you need choose a date, book the hall and set up a range of treatments and therapies. Issue a school newsletter asking if anyone would like to book a place at the event to promote their health and beauty service. Ideally you want to be able to offer pedicures, manicures, nail extensions, massage, spray tanning, reiki, aromatherapy, reflexology etc.

If a letter through school doesn't produce one of each of the services you want to offer, approach local businesses that offer the service. You can make a charge for the booking, say £10 or £15, but make sure the business will have the opportunity to make more at the event than the sum they pay you.

Next you need to book some stalls to allow the ladies to do some shopping. Again, parents at school who have businesses, local retailers, cottage industries and artists are ideal, as are party plan reps or cosmetic companies like Avon. These events are ideal for jewellery makers but try to provide a wide range of products including ideal gifts and cards. You charge the stall holders for their pitch and can also ask them to donate a prize for the raffle. An as-nu designer clothes and accessories stall always goes down well. Advertise through school offering to sell items for people on a 25/75 % split. You can include a fashion show if you have room.

Once you have all your stalls and services booked you can start marketing your event. Print flyers, tickets and even programmes. We usually charged £5 a ticket for admission, which included entry in to a draw and a glass of wine.

Put the beauty and therapy lists up on the school notice board for people to book appointments for their chosen treatment ahead of the evening.

Make sure you have use of some classrooms and screens to make private areas for the therapies and for trying on clothes. Have some background music playing to help create an atmosphere. Organise a bar and some refreshments and make sure you have somewhere for people to sit and socialise.

Your event can include some demonstrations like fitness taster sessions or dance lessons.

It's always nice to send everyone home with a goody bag. As with the dinner dance, if you are able to get the support of a local salon they may provide bags for you; alternatively you can make your own up by contacting manufacturers and asking for free samples of their products to include.

The pamper evening can be as big as you want to make it, the most important thing is to make sure everyone has a good time and that includes the businesses that have paid to be a part of your event.

BEDTIME STORIES

This is an ingenious way to encourage reading and raise money for school. Tickets are sold to pupils for a bedtime story event starting at around 6pm at school on a chosen date. Children are invited to return to school in their pyjamas for a story. Teachers give up an hour of their time to transform their classroom in to a comfortable reading room with soft lighting, cushions and throws. Cookies and milk are served in the classroom before the teacher starts story time. At our school charging £2 for a ticket which provided children with an hour's entertainment and refreshments, could net us in excess of £300 profit.

More funds can be raised by serving refreshments to parents in the school hall once they have dropped the children to their classrooms. While the children enjoy their bedtime story parents and carers relax in the café you have created. You can also set up a book sale or book fair and have outside stalls brought in for which stallholders pay a fee.

A book raffle is another way of increasing your takings.

Finally……

I could carry on writing this book forever but that won't help fundraisers out there, as the book would never be on the shelves for anyone to read. I hope I have provided enough ideas for you to find some new and inspiring fundraising activities.

While more ideas will be added in the second edition of Successful Fundraising for Schools, further fundraising activities will also be detailed on the website. Therefore, there will be no need for anyone who has purchased edition one, to buy edition two as all new ideas will be on the website to keep you updated with further activities and events.

Visit www.fundraisingforschools.co.uk

INDEX

NOTES

NOTES

NOTES

NOTES

www.ingramcontent.com/pod-product-compliance
Lightning Source LLC
Chambersburg PA
CBHW070603290526
45790CB00002B/755